Football
Joke Book

Football
Joke Book

Clive Gifford

WAYLAND

First published in 2014
by Wayland

Copyright © Wayland 2014

Wayland
338 Euston Road
London NW1 3BH

Wayland Australia
Level 17/207 Kent Street
Sydney, NSW 2000

Commissioning Editor: Victoria Brooker
Project Editor: Caroline West
(Blue Dragonfly Ltd.)
Designer: Mark Latter
(Blue Dragonfly Ltd.)
Illustrator: Alan Rowe

A CIP catalogue record for this book is available
from the British Library.
Dewey number: 828.9'202–dc23
ISBN: 978 0 7502 8286 4

Printed by CPI Group (UK) Ltd

Wayland is a division of Hachette Children's Books,
a Hachette UK company.
www.hachettechildrens.co.uk

Contents

Football Players

What do Lionel Messi and a magician have in common?

Both are good at hat tricks.

WORLD CUP FACT!

At the 1938 World Cup, the Italian striker, Giuseppe Meazza, went to take a penalty kick against Brazil when his shorts fell down! Keeping his cool, he hitched his shorts up, scored the penalty and Italy went on to win the World Cup.

How does Cristiano Ronaldo stay cool during hot games at the World Cup?

He stands near the fans!

Did you know that wingers are the only people who can dribble and still look neat?

PLAYER FACT!

Poldi Kielholz played in the 1934 and 1938 World Cup for Switzerland wearing his glasses during games. He managed to score three goals!

Manager: "I call our striker, Dane Mooney, my £10 million wonder player."

Reporter: "Why?"

Manager: "Because every time he plays and misses a goal, I wonder why I paid £10 million for him!"

8

I'm not saying our new midfielder's fat, but every time he falls over in a game, he rocks himself to sleep trying to get up!

A manager is interviewing a possible new player for his team and asks:
"Do you kick with both feet?"
"Don't be silly," **replies the player.**
"If I did that, I wouldn't be able to stand up, would I!"

Our new Spanish midfielder is so keen on staying fit that he works carrying bricks on a building site during the summer?
I didn't know that. What's his name again?
Manuel Labour!

Terrible midfielder: "Boss, I've got a fab idea for making the team better."
Manager: "Great, I didn't know you were leaving!"

Our new striker, Edmundo Cesar Lorenzo Farrincha Gonzalez De Sousa, incurred quite a transfer fee last year. And that was just for his name on the back of the shirt!

**60 million wouldn't buy
Fernando Torres...
and I'm one of them!**

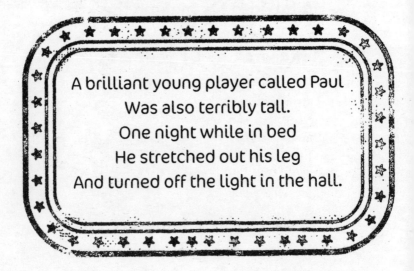

A brilliant young player called Paul
Was also terribly tall.
One night while in bed
He stretched out his leg
And turned off the light in the hall.

**Why do they call the rubbish
midfielder who's been dropped
from the team,
"The Archaeologist"?**

Because his career is in ruins!

There once was a player from Reading
Who tripped and fell over some bedding.
His head really swelled
But he smiled and he yelled,
"Great! This will help me with heading!"

Tricky Winger

The Winger pulled out all of his tricks.

A striker who played for United
Turned out to be very short-sighted.
With great ball control,
He scored an own goal
And the other team's fans were delighted.

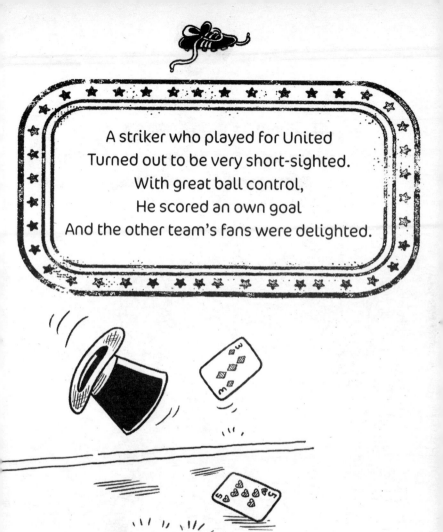

**Why did Cinderella get
dropped from her team?**
Because she was always
running away from the ball.

Reporter: "What happened when the world's smallest man joined your team?"
Manager: "We played the game a man short!"

In football, what's harder
to catch the faster you run?
Your breath!

Sliding Tackle

What do you get if you cross a football player with a mythical creature that has the head of a man and the body of a horse?

A centaur forward

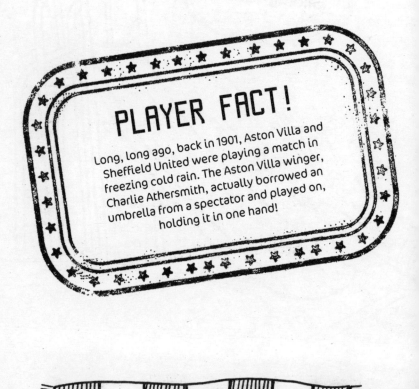

PLAYER FACT!

Long, long ago, back in 1901, Aston Villa and Sheffield United were playing a match in freezing cold rain. The Aston Villa winger, Charlie Athersmith, actually borrowed an umbrella from a spectator and played on, holding it in one hand!

The head coach of the town's struggling
football team was walking down the street
when he saw an old lady puffing as she
dragged her shopping bags along.
He stopped and asked her, "Can you manage?"
She replied, "Of course I can, but you
got yourself into this mess.
Don't ask me to sort it out!"

Coach: Why are you crying, Billy?
Silly striker: Because my new
football boots hurt, boss.
Coach: Doh! That's because you
put them on the wrong feet.
Silly striker: But, they're the only
feet I have, boss.

Which player would you not want to share a room with?
Lionel Messi!

Did you hear about the two hugely overweight players on their first day back in training?
One trained in short bursts and the other trained in burst shorts!

Manager:
You missed wet weather training yesterday, didn't you?

Player:
Not very much!

Gareth Bale has revealed that he left Spurs due to a long-term back injury – brought on by having to carry the rest of his team for so long!

PLAYER FACT!

In 2008, Chippenham Town striker, David Pratt, was sent off for a bad tackle just THREE seconds after the game had begun. Now that's fast!

What happened when the midfielder belched loudly?
The referee awarded a freak hic!

Why did Cinderella not improve as a footballer?
Because her coach turned into a pumpkin!

Did you hear about the Premiership footballer who installed a skylight in his expensive apartment?
The people in the flat above were furious!

Why didn't the short midfielder need much sleep?
He was never long in bed!

Football
Teams

**When our new manager said he thought
our team would finish second this season,
I thought he meant in the league.
I didn't realise that he meant
in every single game!**

TEAM FACT!

The biggest thrashing ever in international
football happened in 2001. Australia and
American Samoa were playing in a qualifying
game for the 2002 World Cup.
Australia won... 31–0.

**Which English football team
likes ice cream the most?**
Aston Vanilla

Ivor Chestikov

Arthur Eyetus

Ian Jury

Ed Ache

Diego Marrow-Donor

Manager Ann Bewlance

Why did Turkey get the most yellow cards?
Because the referee felt they made
the most fowl tackles.

WORLD CUP FACT!

At the 1962 World Cup, the Chilean team ate food that was famous from their opponent's country before they played them. They ate Swiss cheese and beat Switzerland and then dined on spaghetti before beating Italy. Sadly, despite drinking Brazilian coffee, they lost to Brazil in the semi-finals.

**What is a snake's favourite
football team?**
Slitherpool

What's the difference between my football team and a tea bag?

The tea bag stays in the cup longer.

Which side did Shy Barry, Quiet Steve and Wouldn't-Say-Boo-To-A-Goose-Gordon all play for?

The reserve-d team

What colour football kit did the shoutiest and mouthiest team in the league wear?

Yeller!

31

If you were a hermit, which football team would you support?
Barce-loner

Why did all the pigs in the football team stand to attention before the game started?
Because the band started playing the National Hamthem.

Why was the African Game Reserve football team banned?
It was found to be full of cheetahs!

Veteran Player in the Frame

TEAM FACT!

The biggest scoreline in a football match occurred in 2002 in Madagascar, a large island off the coast of Africa. AS Adema beat SO L'Emyrne by a score of....149–0!

33

**Our new striker is scoring hatfuls
of goals in training. Then again, it's
not much of a surprise. After all,
he is playing against his own
team's defence!**

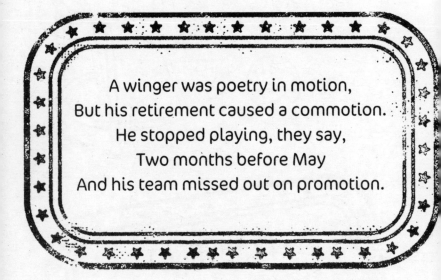

A winger was poetry in motion,
But his retirement caused a commotion.
He stopped playing, they say,
Two months before May
And his team missed out on promotion.

**What football team does the
demolition man like to support?**

Wrexham!

Filthy thieves have stolen the team bath at Arsenal's Emirates Stadium.

Police believe they made a clean getaway!

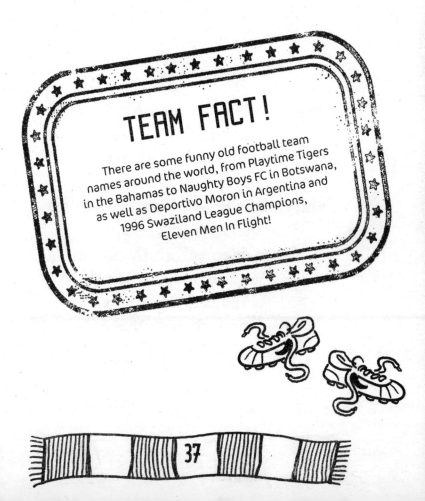

TEAM FACT!

There are some funny old football team names around the world, from Playtime Tigers in the Bahamas to Naughty Boys FC in Botswana, as well as Deportivo Moron in Argentina and 1996 Swaziland League Champions, Eleven Men In Flight!

Which national team's footballers cannot wait for lunch or dinner-time after training?
Hungary!

Snow White goes searching for the football-mad Seven Dwarfs who are believed to be lost in a cave. Reaching the cave's entrance, she shouts down, "Who will win the World Cup this year?"
From deep within the cave comes the reply, "England!"
"Ah," **says Snow White,** "At least Dopey is still alive!"

Team Taunts

We've used some of the Premier League's top teams and their players here, but you can insert the names of teams and players your friends support instead, if you want to!

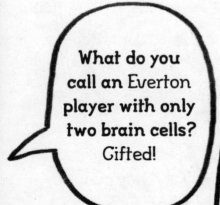

What do you call an Everton player with only two brain cells? Gifted!

I hear Oxo are bringing out a new gravy cube in Liverpool colours. It's called Laughing Stock and crumbles under pressure.

Two football fans were walking through a cemetery when they saw a tombstone that read:
"Here lies Jack Carter –
a good man and a Chelsea fan."
One turned to the other and asked,
"When did they start putting two people in one grave?!"

Goalkeepers and Goals

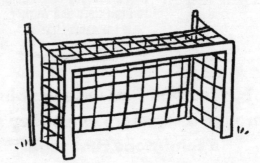

What type of footballer do bank managers like the most?

Goalkeepers. They're the best savers!

GOALKEEPER FACT!

Poor Santiago Cañizares. He was Spain's number one goalkeeper going into the 2002 World Cup before he injured himself. How? He dropped a bottle of aftershave onto his foot. Iker Casillas took his place and became Spain's goalkeeper for the next 10 years!

What do you call a girl who stands inside the goalposts and stops the ball rolling away?

Annette

GOALKEEPER FACT!

In a 1975 match against Birmingham, the Manchester United goalie, Alex Stepney, dislocated his jaw. The cause of his injury? Shouting too hard at his defenders!

44

**I've been asked to sign up as
the new goalkeeper for the
Circus Clown FC team.**
As an amateur?
No, it's a fool-time job!

A real-life chant by Crystal Palace
fans at the Colchester United
goalkeeper, Dean Gerken:
"Stayed in a burger, you should
have stayed in a burger!"

**What's the difference between
a terrible goalkeeper and
a taxi cab driver?**
A taxi cab driver only
lets four in at a time!

Which insect doesn't make a great goalkeeper?

The fumble bee!

**Why was the goalkeeper
nicknamed Dracula?**
Because he was afraid of crosses!

**A famous but not too bright goalkeeper
treated his family to a trip to
Disneyland in California. As he was
driving the car to the theme park,
he saw a sign saying,** "Disneyland Left".
"Oh well," **he sighed and turned the car
round to drive back to the airport!**

My computer's got the
Bad-Goalie Virus.
It can't save anything.

Team captain:
"Why didn't you stop that ball?"
New goalkeeper:
"I thought that's what the net was for!"

Assistant coach:
"Our new striker's terrible, boss.
I thought you said he eats, drinks
and sleeps football."
Head coach: "Yes, he does...
he just can't play it!"

Mary had a little lamb
Who played in goal a lot.
It let in lots and lots of goals,
So now it's in the pot.

Our goalie's useless in the match,
but he makes a great screensaver.

GOALS FACT!

Own goals are when you score a goal by accident against your own team. Poor old Stan Van Den Buys, a defender in the Belgian league. He once scored three own goals in a game to give the other team, Anderlecht, a 3-0 win!

A goalie let in six goals in each of his last three games. Worrying about how badly he's been playing, he goes to see his doctor.

"Your problem is you've got two left feet," diagnoses the doctor.

"I'd like a second opinion," insists the goalie.

"Okay. You're useless, too!" replies the doctor.

Our new goalkeeper's so thick that he once tiptoed past the medicine cabinet at the training ground because he didn't want to wake up the sleeping pills!

WORLD CUP FACT!

Ramón Quiroga was Peru's goalkeeper at the 1978 World Cup. Nicknamed El Loco for his mad behaviour, Quiroga liked to wander out of his penalty area and was once shown a yellow card for tackling an opponent in the other half of the pitch!

What's a goalkeeper's favourite meal?

Beans on post

Our new goalkeeper has just been nicknamed "Jigsaw".

Why's that?

Because every time the other team attacks, he falls to pieces!

Why was the goalkeeper always at the laundrette?

He was hoping to get more clean sheets!

Referees
and
Managers

Where do the chairmen of football clubs go in their grounds during a dull O-O draw?
The Bored Room!

WORLD CUP FACT!

The referee in the first World Cup Final in 1930 didn't wear what you'd expect. No black shirt and shorts for him. Instead, he wore a dinner jacket, tie and horse-riding jodhpurs!

Why was the manager happy to be caught speeding by the traffic police?
He was delighted to get three points!

**What is a referee's
favourite drink?**
Penal-tea!

**A referee shows a yellow card to
a player for a bad foul and says,**
"Ronnie, you really must learn
how to give and take."
The player replies,
"But I have, Ref. I gave him a kick
and took his legs away!"

The England manager has set up
a friendly match for the England team
against Iceland to try and cheer up fans.
If they win that game, they'll play
Tesco next Saturday and then
Asda on Wednesday!

Why did the referee send the vampire off?

For making biting tackles!

Player to manager: "I know I wasn't at my best today, but I don't think I deserve a mark of 0 out of 10 for my performance."

Manager to player: "Neither do I, but it's the lowest mark I can give!"

The new manager of our struggling football team is strict and won't stand any nonsense. Last Saturday, he caught two fans climbing over the stadium wall and was angry with them. He grabbed them and said, "Get back in there and watch the game until it finishes!"

Skipper

Referee: "I'm sending you off."
Player: "What for?"
Referee: "For the rest of the match, dummy!"

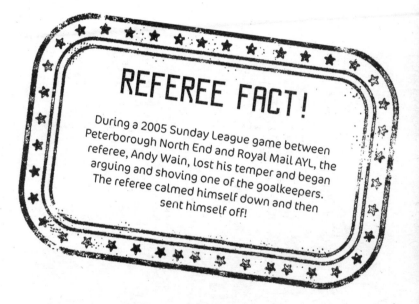

REFEREE FACT!

During a 2005 Sunday League game between Peterborough North End and Royal Mail AYL, the referee, Andy Wain, lost his temper and began arguing and shoving one of the goalkeepers. The referee calmed himself down and then sent himself off!

Assistant coach: "That new player you've signed, boss, only weighs 30kg and only has a 22-inch waist.
Where did you get him from?"
Manager: "Finland!"

Referee to a player:
"I hope I don't see you cheating."
Player to referee:
"I hope you don't see either, Ref!"

Why did the England manager bring pencils and sketchpads into the dressing room before the World Cup game?
He was hoping the England team would draw the match!

"Oi, Sergio," shouted the angry manager in the dressing room. **"You were terrible today. You're a disgrace to the team."**

"Don't listen to him," said a team-mate afterwards, trying to cheer Sergio up. **"He doesn't know what he's talking about. He only repeats what everybody else says!"**

MANAGER FACT!

In a 1999 Spanish Division Two match, a player from the team Badajoz looked like he was going to score until the other team's manager, Enrique Martin, rushed onto the pitch and tackled him. Martin was banned for 10 games as a result.

The Kitty

**Why did the struggling
manager shake the club cat?**

To see if there was any money
for transfers left in the kitty!

Fans and Football Grounds

Why did the football pitch end up in the shape of a triangle?

Because a player took a corner!

FAN FACT!

In 2011, mad-keen Swansea City fan, Michael Rees, painted his entire house in his football club's colours. No, he wasn't a football-crazy teenager. Michael was 69 years old!

Where do giant killer plants play football?

Old Triffid!

**At which ground do
spiders play football?**
Webley Stadium!

A not-too-bright football fan arrives
really late and takes his seat during
the second half of the game.
"What's the score?"
he asks as he sits down.
"Nil-Nil," the person next to him replies.
**"And what was the score
at half-time?"** he asks.

**What flies at a football ground
but doesn't go anywhere?**
A corner flag!

The Transfer Window is Open

FAN FACT!

During the 2009/10 football season, a thick fog fell on the game between Colchester United and Southampton. The Colchester fans started singing near the end of the match:
"We can't see you sneaking out!"

A football fan hands over £40 to the ticket office at Stoke City FC and says,
"Two please."
The ticket person replies,
"Will that be defenders or strikers, sir?"

A football fan appears in court charged with throwing something into the river.
Judge: "And what did you throw?"
Fan: "Wood."
Judge: "Well, that's not much of a crime is it?"
Lawyer: "Ahem, your lordship, Wood was the referee."

Two fans are in the queue to
get into the grounds...

I wish I'd brought
my bedroom table
to the stadium.

Why would you
do that?

Because I left our
tickets on it.

**How many sides are there to
our new football stadium?**
Two. The inside and the outside!

What do you call a football pitch groundsman with a spade in his hand?

Doug

FAN FACT!

When Udinese played Sampdoria in Italy's top league in 2012, Arrigo Brovedani travelled 500km to support his team, only to discover that he was the only Udinese fan to turn up! The opposing fans cheered him for his loyalty and he was presented with a free football shirt.

"I hear they're making improvements for the fans at your ground... They're turning all the seats round so that they face away from the pitch."

Which month of the
football season has
28 days?

All of them... idiot!

"This pitch is soaking wet,"
said the football groundsman.
**"That's because the players have
been dribbling all over it,"**
replied the manager.

**What runs along a football
pitch but never moves?**
A sideline!

A man knocked on the door and was asking for donations for his football club's new swimming pool. So, I gave him a glass of water.

Why is an orchestra conductor like 20,000 fans leaving a stadium at the end of a match?
Because they both know the score.

A pound coin was thrown onto the pitch at my struggling football club. Police are trying to work out whether it was thrown by a hooligan or was actually a takeover bid!

Why can't I buy a tea or coffee at this football ground?

Because all the mugs are on the pitch and all the cups are in other teams' trophy cabinets!

What tree can't you climb at a football ground?

A lavatory!

WORLD CUP FACT!

As he was trotting out of the Maracana Stadium for a 1950 World Cup game, Yugoslavia's Rajko Mitic cut his head on a low beam. Because there were no substitutes, Yugoslavia had to start the game with 10, not 11, men. Mitic joined his teammates later on but they lost. Later in the tournament a record 199,850 fans crammed into the stadium to watch Brazil v Uruguay!

Matches and Competitions

Where do Champions League players like to have a dance? At the Champions League Foot Ball, of course!

MATCH FACT!

The first African Cup of Nations competition in 1957 only attracted three countries – Ethiopia, Sudan and the winners, Egypt!

"Oh, I could kick myself," said the striker after failing to score another simple chance.

"Don't bother," replied his captain.

"You'd only miss!"

**Why isn't the England team
allowed to have a dog at
football tournaments?**
Because it can't hold
on to a lead!

Which country at the World Cup
has the slipperiest attackers?
Greece!

**What's the difference between a
saucepan made of chocolate and
the worst team in the league?**
Nothing. They're both pointless!

What did the referee say to the South American footballer who lied about handling the ball?
I don't Bolivia!

Why are the players in my football team like cannons in a battle in every match they play?
Because they keep on getting fired!

Which is the coldest country to take part in the World Cup?
Chile!

MATCH FACT!

Woolpack Wanderers and Garrison Gunners take part in the world's smallest football league on the Isles of Scilly. The two teams play each other 17 times in the league and in two cup competitions as well!

Dead Ball Situation

What's the loudest noise after England take part in a World Cup penalty shootout?

Their opponents laughing!

WORLD CUP FACT!

The World Cup trophy was stolen in 1966 from a stamp exhibition in London! Seriously. Everyone was in a panic until the trophy was discovered a week later under a hedge in South London by a black-and-white collie dog called Pickles. He became a national hero and even starred in a film the following year.

**My team has lost all 11 games
in the league, so what's the difference
between them and a toothpick?**

The toothpick has two points.

WORLD CUP FACT!

At the 2010 World Cup, a German octopus named Paul wowed German football fans. Appearing on TV, Paul the octopus had to choose between two boxes of food to predict the winner of each of the German team's World Cup games. Paul got all seven games right, including Germany's defeat to Spain in the semi-final.

Which World Cup team's players never
carry any cash with them?
The Czechs!

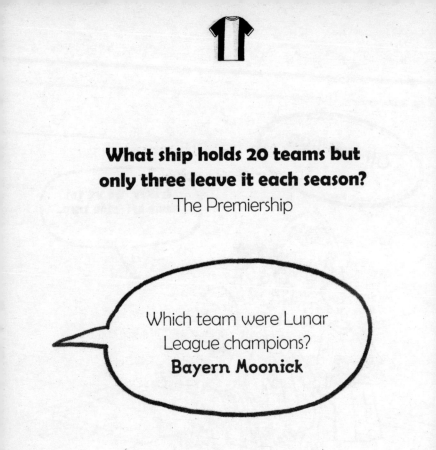

**What ship holds 20 teams but
only three leave it each season?**
The Premiership

Which team were Lunar
League champions?
Bayern Moonick

**"It looks like FC Trifle are
going down this season."**
"Yes, they're going to be jelly-gated!"

What's the Spanish team's favourite scoreline?

Juan-Nil to them!

Football pundits estimate that struggling team Hapless FC will last three seasons in the Premier League... Autumn, Winter and Spring!

Which team is always there at the end of the match?

The Finnish team

FIFA's Funny Football Library

Zero Out of Ten: Rating the Worst Teams of All Time **by A. Pauline Marx**

Football Conditions in Brazil in Summer by Gloria Swether

The Bad Shot by Misty Target

Famous English Football Grounds by Emma Rates and Anne Field

Disaster in Defence **by Owen Goal**

Hurricane Hits Stadium Rufus Blownoff

Cheered Off The Pitch **by Stan D. Novation**

94

A Who's Who of Football
by Hugh Didwatt

Washing Smelly Football Kit
by Dee Tergent

When Fans Snub Stadiums
by M. T. Ground

The Day My Football
Shorts Fell Down
by Lou Selastic

Best Seats in the Stadium
by Sue Perview

MALPAS

They think it's all over...

it is now!